Food For the Greedy

This small volume, filled with delicious and unusual recipes, is perfect for any cook who wishes to prepare beautiful foods using ingredients of the highest quality. *Food for the Greedy* includes only those recipes which are unlikely to be found in other books, permitting epicures and bold chefs to sample such dishes as Haddock Monte Carlo, Basque Kidney Potatoes, Marina Pudding, Iced Pineapple and Cranberry Sauce, and Peach and Ginger Salad. First published in the inter-war years, the book's numerous sauces, salads, soups, meat dishes, vegetables, puddings and cakes are a welcome break from modern cookery book fare.

www.Routledge.com

Food For the Greedy

Nancy Shaw

R Routledge
Taylor & Francis Group

LONDON AND NEW YORK

First published in 2005 by
Kegan Paul International

This edition first published in 2010 by
Routledge
2 Park Square, Milton Park, Abingdon, Oxfordshire OX14 4RN

Simultaneously published in the USA and Canada
by Routledge
711 Third Avenue, New York, NY 10017

First issued in paperback 2016

Routledge is an imprint of the Taylor & Francis Group, an informa business

British Library Cataloguing in Publication Data
A catalogue record for this book is available from the British Library

ISBN 13: 978-1-138-97444-9 (pbk)
ISBN 13: 978-0-7103-1044-6 (hbk)

Publisher's Note
The publisher has gone to great lengths to ensure the quality of this reprint
but points out that some imperfections in the original copies may be
apparent. The publisher has made every effort to contact original copyright
holders and would welcome correspondence from those they have been
unable to trace.

Contents

Introduction

THE RECEIPTS which I have assembled in this small book
are ones which I use regularly in my own home. I think
that, at any rate, half of the receipts could not be met with
elsewhere, as I have collected them for many years, from
many people, in many lands. I have so often been asked
for copies of them by my friends that I thought it well
—for their sakes and for my own !—to put a collection of
them into book form.

The receipts are perfectly simple to make but demand
a knowledge of the rudiments of cooking. I have not
attempted to include receipts for the fundamentals—*e.g.*
Béchamel Sauce, Panade, etc.—which are to be found in
every other cookery book.

The first edition of this book was published in 1936,
and has been out of print since before the war. The
present edition contains some new receipts, and I have
omitted one or two which have been copied into other
cookery books. During the last few years there have been
many enquiries for my book, and this is one reason why I
have been persuaded to bring out a new edition.

Even in austerity days I have found these dishes are
well worth the trouble they take to make, and if all the
ingredients are not always readily available there is an
added zest to be enjoyed in making the very best of the
good things that can be got. It is wonderful what a
little ingenuity will do even if all the correct ingredients
are not always easy to obtain.

September, 1951   *Nancy Shaw*

SOUPS AND SAUCES

Potassium Soup

CUT UP SMALL: 3 carrots, 2 onions, 1 large head of celery, ⅛ can of okra and 1 kernel of garlic, and place them in 2 quarts of water. Boil for 17 minutes. Then add 1 handful of parsley and 1 green pepper, and boil again for 7 minutes. Add a large tin of tomatoes and boil up again. Strain through a sieve to the desired thickness.

American receipt, said to ensure longevity!

The "Okra" can be bought at good class grocers who stock less well known canned goods.

From Lord Cobham

Very Good Pot Au Feu

REMOVE THE BONE from 3 lbs. of lean beef (shin, breast or topside) and tie up with string. Break the bones up and place them with the meat in a large saucepan, earthenware if you have it, with 3 quarts of cold water and a dessertspoonful of salt.

Bring slowly to the boil, and remove all scum. Then add 2 carrots, 1 turnip cut in large pieces, 1 large or 2 small onions stuck with 4 cloves (parsnip or celery can be added), one cabbage cut into 4 or 6 pieces, a blade of mace, 15 peppercorns and allspice, and a small bundle of savoury herbs, including parsley.

Put on the lid, and simmer (not boil) for not less than four hours.

The soup should be poured into a tureen in which rather thick slices of stale bread have been placed—1 for each person.

The meat should be served as a separate dish with the vegetables. The quantity of meat given is enough for 8 or 9 persons, the soup for 5 or 6 persons. The meat is excellent cold.

Caramel Cream Sauce

BOIL 3 OZS. SUGAR to a caramel, add a few drops of
lemon juice and pour *boiling* over a small cup of cream.
Leave till cold. Whip another cup of cream and add to
the caramel when cold. Pour over the pudding.
Delicious over any cold cream pudding or soufflé.

From Mrs. George McClintock

Sauce Chôron

REDUCE OVER the fire 1 tablespoonful of vinegar, with
some crushed peppercorns and some tarragon and a little
celery to flavour—or celery salt.

Allow to cool, and add yolks of 3 eggs, 2 tablespoons
of water and a pinch of salt.

Put the whole in a double saucepan on the fire. Keep
whipping hard to obtain a firm creamy consistency.

Take off the fire and add 7 ozs. of warm melted butter.
Stir the whole well to get a firm cream. If too firm, add a
few drops of warm water. Next add a spoonful of tomato
sauce. Pass the whole through a very fine muslin. *Again*
well mix, and finish by seasoning with paprika or cayenne
pepper, salt, juice of one lemon, finely chopped tarragon
and parsley.

Serve just warm. Do not heat too much, to avoid the
butter rising to the top.

The sauce may be served with grilled dishes, poached
or hard-boiled eggs.

Brown Curry Sauce

PEEL AND CHOP a medium-sized onion, put it into a
stewpan with 1 oz. of butter, stir for 5 minutes, then add
two teaspoonfuls of flour, 1 oz. curry powder or paste
mixed well. Moisten with ½ pint of stock or milk, add
pinch of salt, boil till rather thick, pass through a sieve,
make hot and serve.

Iced Sauce for Cold Asparagus

PUT 3 YOLKS of eggs into a saucepan with a pat of butter, pepper and salt to season, and ¼ pint of cream. Cook all this slowly, and on no account boil, whisking all the time. Let it get cool, and add ¼ pint of good thick cream, well whipped, and a tablespoonful of French vinegar. Ice it well.

Iced Sauce for Duck or Gosling

GRATE A HORSERADISH and add to it the strained juice of an orange with 3 tablespoons of salad oil, a table-spoon of vinegar, a coffeespoon of sugar and of salt. Finally some panade is stirred in, which you have already made of very fine breadcrumbs. Add butter, salt, pepper and a little water, work well over the fire, and allow to cool—and at the last moment, just before icing, mix in the grated rind of the orange and freeze.

Iced Sauce for Fish

NO ICED SAUCE must be frozen solid. It must only be half-frozen and easy to serve from the sauce-boat.

For cold fish, turbot especially, the following is excellent and very simple : Take a couple of hard-boiled yolks of eggs. Work with a wooden spoon into a smooth paste with olive oil, French mustard, chopped parsley, chervil, minced gherkins and capers, salt and pepper. At the last, just before freezing, add the whites of the eggs finely sliced.

Sauce for Chicken or Veal

TAKE A GLASS of port wine. Stir in 2 or 3 tablespoons of red currant jelly, juice of an orange, the grated rind of the orange, finely minced shallots, and a teaspoonful of made mustard. Work all very well together and freeze.

Sauce for Grilled Chicken

CHOP A LITTLE onion and cook it in butter. Add the yolks of 2 eggs and cook slowly until it thickens. Then add 1 oz. of butter, a gill of cream and a little melted meat glaze.

Sea Kale Sauce

MAKE ½ PINT of creamy, melted butter sauce, using milk and no water, and season well with salt and pepper and cayenne, and keep warm till required.

Mince your shallots and put them in a small saucepan with ¼ pint of white wine, vinegar and tarragon vinegar mixed in equal quantities. Boil quickly till the original measure is reduced to a tablespoonful. Then stir in by degrees the white sauce, and when this is thoroughly mixed with the vinegar add the yolks of 3 eggs, whisking each separately into the sauce. Take the saucepan from the stove and add 3 ozs. of butter, which has been cut up into small pieces the size of a walnut, and see that each piece is thoroughly blended with the sauce before another is added, or when finished it will be oily instead of rich and creamy. Strain the sauce and with it mask the sea kale, which has been carefully cooked and most carefully drained. Serve on a hot dish.

Sefton Sauce

MAKE A GOOD mayonnaise of 2 yolks of eggs, breaking them into a bowl. Add by degrees 1 tablespoonful of *tarragon vinegar*, 4 tablespoonfuls of salad oil, and stir till thick. *Then* add 1 stick of grated horseradish, 1 teaspoonful of *common vinegar*, 1 tablespoonful of Worcester sauce, a teaspoonful of anchovy sauce, and 1 gill of whipped cream. Stir well together. Put into a freezing-pot or refrigerator. Freeze till firm. Then serve round all kinds of cold fish, such as trout, salmon, sole, turbot, and cod.

From W. Frith, Chef, Windham Club

Tarragon Cream

SEASON SOME thick cream with salt and pepper, and a dust of curry powder; and whip it until thick. Then flavour it by adding gradually a few drops of white tarragon vinegar. Place it on ice for a short time before serving in a sauce-boat, with cold asparagus.

Tomato Sauce

CUT UP ABOUT 6 tomatoes, put them into a saucepan with 1 oz. of butter, and ½ an onion cut in slices. Stew gently and until tender, then add a little flour, moisten with a little stock, boil up for 5 or 6 minutes, strain through a sieve and put it back into the stewpan and simmer until rather thick.

Notes

Notes

Notes

FISH

Baked Crabs in Shell

PICK THE MEAT from half a dozen small boiled crabs in as large pieces as possible. Mix the meat with half its quantity of fresh mushrooms, peeled and cut into small pieces. Season with salt and pepper, and moisten with melted butter.

Put into the cleaned crab shells, and over each sprinkle some fine breadcrumbs and grated parmesan cheese.

Place in a hot oven to bake for ¼ hour.

Cook the mushrooms in butter a little before chopping and putting into the shells.

Crab Mayonnaise

PICK OUT ALL the meat from some cooked crabs, size according to what quantity is required (do not mix in the soft brown cream of the crab).

Cut up little langoustines or Dublin Bay prawns in small pieces. Mix all with salt and red pepper. Arrange on a dish with a crisp undressed lettuce round, and serve with a very good creamy mayonnaise sauce, whipped cream being added to the mayonnaise.

Haddock Monte Carlo

FILLET 1 SMOKED HADDOCK of 1 lb. Put the fillets in an earthenware dish with 2 fresh tomatoes, peeled and cut in slices. Add 6 tablespoonfuls of fresh cream, and 2 ozs. of butter. Cook in a hot oven for about 10 minutes, or until the fish is properly cooked. Serve at once.

Creamed Smoked Haddock

TAKE A LARGE smoked haddock and boil it in milk very

slowly, till well cooked. Remove skin and bone, and flake the fish fairly small, and mix into a very good Béchamel sauce, finished off with thick cream. Cook thoroughly and serve if possible in a double dish, with the fish one side and carefully boiled rice in the other. The haddock cream must not be stiff but creamy.

I find this is always much liked for a first course at lunch.

To Cook Halibut, Sole or Grey Mullet

LAY THE FISH in a buttered tin or fireproof oval dish. Cut in slices a carrot and small onion, a faggot of parsley, thyme, and 4 bay leaves, and place over the fish.

Add a pint of good stock, 2 tablespoonfuls of salad oil, a small spoonful of anchovy paste, and the juice of 1 lemon.

Cover the dish with a sheet of paper, and put it into a *slow* oven for 20 minutes, basting frequently.

Then strain off the gravy, and thicken with a small tablespoonful of flour, to the consistency of cream. Then add some chopped cooked mushrooms and a little wine. Heat this and pour over the fish.

This sauce can be made separately and served in a sauce boat with any kind of fish.

Jellied Eels

TAKE 3 EELS, skinned, cut them in longish pieces, wash them well. Put in stewpan with 3 pints water, 1 small cup tarragon vinegar, 1 onion finely cut up, 1 small carrot, 1 clove, 6 peppercorns, 1 teaspoonful salt, and a bouquet of herbs (bunch of parsley, 2 bay leaves, 1 bunch thyme, tied together). When boiling, add 8 leaves of powered gelatine, previously soaked for a few minutes, or 3 tablespoons of powdered gelatine, and then let simmer for 20 minutes on side of stove. Then take eels out of the broth, put in a deep dish and *strain* the broth over them. Put in a cool place to set, when they are ready.

Lobster Creams

TAKE THE MEAT from the shell of a lobster, size depending on how many creams are wanted. Chop the meat small and then put in a mortar with essence of anchovy and cayenne pepper to taste.

Pound all this to a paste, pouring in by degrees, to the paste, some stiffly whipped cream, until you make the paste to the consistency of thickish custard.

Serve in cups or small very cold bowls, and serve thin dry toast with them.

A first-course lunch dish.

Lobster Newberg

GET YOUR CHAFING-DISH and see that the water in the receptacle boils. Then put a cupful of cream in the pan, and as soon as it is heated add the beaten yolks of three eggs, gradually stirring all the time. When the sauce has thickened, add two cupsful of chopped fresh boiled lobster and half a cupful of sherry, stirring all the while, and seasoning with pepper and salt to taste. Serve as soon as the lobster is heated through, but on no account allow it to boil.

"Lobster Newberg" derives its name from its inventor, Ben Wenberg. He was a regular habitué of Delmonico's and one of the men who made popular the chafing-dish. Charles Delmonico once put lobster cooked after his special receipt on the bill of fare as : " Lobster à la Wenberg." The inventor's objections to this were so strong that this delectable dish has ever since borne his name reversed : " Lobster à la Newberg."

The old Delmonico's formula for lobster Newberg

19

A Lobster Newberg with Rice Pilaff

TAKE A BOILED LOBSTER and cut the flesh into rounds. Dip them in melted butter and put in sauté pan and pour madeira or sherry over. Set light to them, and let cook a few minutes. Beat well the yolk of 1 or 2 eggs (according to quantity of lobster) with a cupful of cream, and add a little more of the wine previously used. Add salt and paprika, and put into pan with the lobster. Keep on shaking all well together till the sauce thickens and is very hot, but is not boiling. (The sauce must be like very thick cream.) Serve very hot with *Rice Pilaff*.

Parboil, then chop onion in 2 ozs. of butter and let the onion brown slightly. Add ½ lb. of Italian rice (which is unbleached rice). Have about 1 pint of chicken stock, add this to the rice and also half a dozen prawns. Cook all till rice is soft and has absorbed the stock, about 20 minutes.

Rice with Lobster

THE RICE IS BOILED in the ordinary way and formed to a ring shape in a mould. The meat of 2 lobsters is cut in small pieces. The shell is pounded in a mortar together with some butter. When the mixture is quite fine, it is put in a saucepan with boiling water. After a little while the red butter rises to the surface and is skimmed off. This butter is fried in a saucepan with a little flour, and some thick cream added so that it becomes a thick sauce. The red roe is added. The pieces of lobster are put in and a little cayenne pepper added, and also a small glass of whisky. The rice ring is filled with the stew and makes a delicious lunch dish. Pounding the shell of the lobster to a paste gives a fine flavour to the lobster stew, and the whisky is most important.

Swedish receipt from Mrs. Swanberg

Sole à la Crème

TAKE SOME FILLETS of sole, dry them with a cloth, and put into a well-buttered baking dish (fireproof).

Pour enough cream almost to fill the shallow dish, and then add about a teaspoonful of anchovy essence (enough to flavour and turn the cream slightly pink, but not to make it too salt).

Bake in a moderate oven for about half an hour.

It is better to put a greased paper over the dish till cooked, and then remove it and let the top brown a little.

The sauce should be like very thick cream.

Soufflé of Sole

TAKE ONE LARGE SOLE, fillet and skin it and pound it very well, adding about 1 tablespoon of Panard. (This is made by boiling ¼ pint of water with a pinch of salt and ½ oz. of butter, and, when it is boiling, by sifting in 2 tablespoonfuls of fine flour and cooking it on the stove for about 5 minutes, stirring to keep it smooth and to prevent it from catching. When ready it should be thick enough to ball.) After adding the Panard, pound again for a few minutes, add 2 eggs and pass through a fine sieve. Mix about 1½ gills of whipped cream and the whites of 2 eggs beaten very stiff. Fill up soufflé case with layers of this mixture, also sliced cooked lobster and button mushrooms that have been cooked in butter. Steam for ¾ of an hour.

From Mr. Howard Reed

Sole Whitehall

BOIL ENOUGH spaghetti to fill ¾ of your casserole, in salted water for about 20 minutes. Strain and season with pepper and salt, and a pat of butter. Have some fat bacon cut in small dices, cook in oven, also mushrooms chopped fine and cooked in oven in butter.

Take a filleted sole, cut each fillet lengthway in half, so that you have 8 pieces. Wipe them and flour them well and fry in fresh lard a nice pale colour. Mix all well together and put in oven to get thoroughly hot and the fats to melt.

You can also poach oysters and put on top. The stew must be rather buttery.

Three 1 lb. soles, 1 lb. mushrooms and ¾ lb. fat bacon are enough for 10 people.

Tunny Fish Soufflé

TAKE A SMALL tin of tunny, and put the contents to drain off all the oil, and run boiling water over it in the colander.

Mix a piece of butter, the size of an egg, in a saucepan together with 3 heaped-up dessertspoonfuls of flour. When well mixed and beginning to colour, add boiling milk in small quantities, stirring over the fire till the whole mixture is as thick as a liquid potato purée. Remove saucepan from the fire, mix in 3 yolks of eggs, then add your tunny fish minced finely. The 3 whites of eggs, well beaten up, are now added and some spoonfuls of ham chopped. Pour the whole mixture into a soufflé dish and cook in a hot oven for 30 minutes.

Whiting à l'Anglaise

SPLIT SEVERAL whiting open and bone them. Dip in flour and then into melted butter. Now roll them in the finest breadcrumbs. Arrange on a fireproof dish, laying several tiny pieces of butter on each. Cook slowly under the grill until they are a nice delicate brown. Send up a good thin white sauce, flavoured with a "fumet" or essence of fish made from the fish trimmings.

From the Ivy Restaurant

Notes

Notes

LUNCH OR SUPPER DISHES
A Summer First-Course Dish

TAKE HARD-BOILED EGGS, cut in small pieces, and same quantity of shelled shrimps. Mix up with a good cream mayonnaise sauce. Make very cold and serve with sandwiches of brown bread and mustard and cress.

From Sophy, Lady Hall

A Basque Receipt—for a Winter's-day Lunch

TAKE A HUGE POTATO, stand it lengthways and cut a hole that will hold a small kidney, but keeping as much as possible of the potato, including the top. Take a lamb kidney, which has been cut out of the fat, leaving some of the fat on it. Put into the potato, with a little salt and pepper, then put on the top. Tie up with string so as to keep the top down, and very slowly bake in oven till the potato is cooked. Remove string and send to table. When the little top is removed, the potato is filled with a delicious cooked kidney and the potato full of gravy. This dish is a meal in itself.

From Mr. Gerald Brockhurst, R.A.

Petites Caisses

LINE SOME small moulds with strong meat jelly, and in each of these place a cube of foie gras truffle. Cover with more of the jelly, and place on ice until set.

Turn out and serve garnished with finely chopped jelly, and salad in the centre.

The Wiltshire Dish of Bacon and Broad Beans

TAKE A PIECE of home-cured bacon, about 5 or 6 lbs. Soak it in water overnight. The next day put it into a deep saucepan of cold water and boil up and then let it go on simmering. The time to allow for cooking is 20 minutes for every pound of bacon and 20 minutes over. Half an hour before it is cooked, take sufficient broad beans for a dish and put it with the bacon and finish the cooking, as ¼ an hour is enough for the beans.

Caneton Bigarade

PLACE THE DUCK in a casserole or stewpan with a knob of butter and roast for 20 minutes.

Remove the duck and swill the stewpan with a wineglass of Orange Curaçao and a wineglass of port wine.

Let this reduce well and then add 1¼ gills of glaze and a gill of sauce Diable (Escoffier). Also add the juice of 2 oranges. Let the sauce cook for 25 minutes, and then add a dessertspoonful of red currant jelly. Pass the sauce through a hair sieve. It is then ready for serving.

Place the duck in the centre of dish and surround it with quarters of oranges.

The peel of the oranges and also the peel of 2 lemons should then be cut into a fine julienne and blanched and sprinkled over the duck.

Pour half of the sauce over the duck and serve very hot. The rest of the sauce can be served separately.

From Mr. Howard Reed

A Cold Egg Dish

FRY PIECES OF French roll in butter. Poach as many eggs as are required, and having drained them well, put them on the rounds of toast.

Make some rich mayonnaise sauce to which you have added cream. Now you have some ham cut in the very thinnest possible slices. Pile the ham up in the middle of your dish. Put round and about some anchovies, jelly, and minced hard-boiled white of egg.

The eggs should then have a good cold glaze sauce

poured over them, which you can make by reducing some stock to the thickness of jelly, or else a little meat glaze can be used. Put these eggs round your pile of ham and pour over all the mayonnaise sauce, with little heaps of asparagus (when in season) between the eggs.

This dish must be served very cold.

Eggs Gratin

BRAISE SOME RICE in good stock till brown and very dry. Boil some eggs soft, and having then shelled them by first plunging into cold water, lay them on top. Pour over these a Hollandaise sauce. Sprinkle well with parmesan cheese and put under the grill for a few minutes to brown.

The sauce is made as follows :

Put a ¼ lb. of butter into a basin with 3 yolks of eggs, and salt, and a tablespoon of vinegar, and let this stand for 4 hours. Then when sauce is wanted, stand the basin in a saucepan of boiling water and whip up until the sauce is like very thick cream. This is enough for a dish of 6 eggs.

Eggs and Rice

A BED OF well-cooked rice with either poached eggs, or soft-boiled eggs, left whole and shell removed, with the following sauce all over is a good simple lunch dish.

Sauce : Small piece of butter in saucepan, very small teaspoonful of fécule of potatoes (Groult's preparations). Stir together well over the fire. Then add a little hot water, and when mixed, stir in several big spoonfuls of cream. If the sauce is not thick enough, add a little more fécule.

Eggs Rosebery

SCRAMBLE EGGS and mix in any remains of cold salmon, adding salt and pepper. The dish, if properly made, should

reproduce Lord Rosebery's racing colours : viz., primrose
and rose. It looks pretty and tastes delicious!

From Lord Cobham

Oeufs Brouillés en Gelée

SCRAMBLE THE EGGS in the usual way, well-seasoned
and of a creamy consistency. Let them get icy cold. Have
ready a good aspic jelly made of very good stock, either
chicken or consommé. Put a layer of jelly in the bottom
of the dish, then the eggs, finishing with more jelly on the
top : garnish to taste, and serve.

Cold Mousse of Eggs

FIVE HARD-BOILED EGGS, ½ pint lightly-whipped
cream, 4 tablespoonfuls stiff aspic; pepper, salt and a little
paprika—Harvey, Worcester and anchovy sauces to taste.

Pass the yolks through a fine sieve, *chop* the whites.

Mix all the seasoning with the *sieved yolks*, then add aspic.
Let it set for a little, then add the whipped cream, and last
of all the chopped whites.

Pour into a soufflé dish and let get thoroughly cold.

Quantity for 8 people. Put some chopped aspic on the
top and a little chopped parsley—green mayonnaise sauce
served with it.

From Mrs. Basil Buckley

Green Omelette

BREAK 3 EGGS into a basin and 3 eggs into another basin.
Pour nearly ½ pint of cream, equally divided, into each
basin. Add to one ¼ lb. spinach that has been boiled and
passed through a hair sieve. Cook both mixtures separately
in omelette pan and turn into dish side by side. Pour
over a good sauce of gravy, slightly thickened with arrow-

root, or better still a tomato sauce round the omelette, not over it.

I find this omelette is rather too rich with only cream. It is really better to put some milk with the cream.

Spaghetti and Eggs *A First-Course Lunch Dish*

BOIL SOME SPAGHETTI in salted water. Drain well. Hard boil 4 eggs, or more according to size of dish required, and skin some tomatoes. Take a fireproof dish, put in a layer of spaghetti, then a layer of tomatoes sliced, and then a layer of hard-boiled eggs cut in slices; and repeat this till dish is filled. You can put in a little onion if liked.

Now have a very good Béchamel sauce, flavoured with parmesan cheese and made with some cream, and fill up the dish, covering the contents. Sprinkle a little parmesan on top. Put into oven and bake till all is well heated through and the sauce has became a golden brown on top.

When properly done, the contents of dish must come out all soft and creamy. On no account must it be stiff or dry.

Mixed Grill with Smoked Haddock

THIS IS RATHER different from the ordinary mixed grill, and I find it much liked for a lunch party.

Take a good-sized finnan-haddock, and having boned it, cook in a buttered dish in milk. When cooked, take out and drain, as the milk gets too salt, and put into fireproof dish. Lay slices of streaky bacon (that you have already cooked crisp in oven) across the fillets of haddock, and then round them put grilled lamb kidneys (that have been sent with the fat round them) cut into slices, small grilled lamb cutlets and mushrooms, pieces of chicken, and anything else that grills well. Must be sent up very hot, with just enough butter to prevent looking dry.

Forced mushrooms require more cooking than the field variety which are no trouble as they soften directly: the best way of dealing with forced ones is to leave the skins on them. Keeping skins uppermost pour over them two or three kettles of boiling water before proceeding with the real cooking (this tenderises them and helps to preserve the flavour). A good way to cook them is to put them in a tin (with a good piece of butter) in the oven and slowly cook until they are quite soft.

Sauce: Take ⅓ bottle of Escoffier Derby sauce, add ⅓ teaspoon powdered mustard, a little Worcester sauce and some cream. Mix over fire and serve hot. This quantity is enough for 4 persons.

Ragout of Mutton Berbere

CUT THE mutton in pieces and follow this method:

Cut meat into cubes about 1½ inches square, brown in olive oil (be generous with oil) and after browning put on one side. Mince 2 lbs. onions, browning slightly in olive oil. Mix onions and mutton together in the olive oil and add enough water (hot) to make plenty of juice for immersing.

The following spices to be added:—generous quantity of powdered paprika, small quantity of saffron, a pinch of curry powder, a pinch of cinnamon, a good pinch of powdered cummin, a pinch of powdered cloves, thyme, bay leaves 2 or 3 and wild parsley—(not ordinary parsley or taste ruined). Add a few turnips and carrots and one good nut of garlic.

This must be simmered for at least two hours. If a whole leg of mutton is used without cutting up, more liquid must be used. Dried apricots, previously soaked should be put in the dish half-an-hour before end of cooking.

Be generous with all herbs and spices. Boiled potatoes can be served with this dish.

Made by the Berbers near Casa Blanca

Smoked Haddock Soufflé

TAKE ONE smoked Haddock, and pass through a sieve, or chop very finely. Boil the fish bones to make the sauce. Put butter in pan to melt, and after adding flour, cook over a low heat; add milk and stock from bones to make a fairly thick sauce. Bring to the boil, stirring all the time. Add the fish, mix well in with the sauce, and add 3 or 4 yolks of egg, (according to the quantity of fish). Beat the whites and fold into the mixture. Pour into the soufflé dish; and bake for about ½ to ¾ of an hour in a fairly hot oven. Serve immediately.

Brown Nut Fish

MAKE EVEN size cutlets of Cod or Hake or other white fish. Wipe them, removing skins and centre bone. Place in a well buttered dish, sprinkle with a little curry powder, chopped capers and chopped blanched almonds. Season well and put small pieces of butter on them, laying tiny pieces of bacon on top.

Bake in moderate oven for about 20 minutes, basting every now and then. Sprinkle with bread crumbs and return to the oven to crisp the crumbs for about 5 minutes. Serve in hot dish.

Red Mullet

SCRAPE ALL SCALES off the fish. Pour a generous measure of lemon juice over them. Place into a fireproof dish with finally chopped garlic and a little *oil* and place under the grill. Grill first one side of the fish then turn and do the other. When cooked, take from fire and put some finely chopped parsley over them. Serve immediately.

Fillets of Sole à la Meuniere

ONE 1½ LB. Sole filleted. Five thin rashers streaky Bacon. 3 oz. butter, 2 large oranges, 1 teaspoonful chopped mixed herbs or parsley, juice of a lemon.

Slice the pith and rind from oranges, cut fruit into sections put them between two plates to keep warm. Lightly flour and season the fillets. Heat a frying pan and drop in 2 oz. butter, when frothing lay in the fillets and fry golden brown, turning once only. Then arrange down a dish for serving with grilled rashers of bacon between each fillet and garnish with orange. Strain the fat from frying pan and drop in the remainder of the butter, when frothing, quickly add the Lemon Juice, herbs and seasoning and pour over dish. *Serve at once.*

Other garnishes may be used instead of oranges :— Artichokes, Celeriac, mushrooms, etc.

Fillets of Fish, with Mushrooms

WASH 4 FILLETS of Plaice, Lemon Sole or slices of Hake. Lay them in a buttered fire-proof dish, season with salt, fresh ground pepper, and a few drops of lemon juice. Cover closely with a greased paper and bake in a moderate oven 10 to 15 minutes.

Slice 2 ozs. washed mushrooms also finely minced. Place in a small saucepan with pinch of salt, little pepper, fragment of butter and *water barely to cover.*

Bring to the boil, cover pan and cook gently for 5 minutes and then draw off liquor.

Sauce : Whilst fish and mushrooms are cooking, melt in

32

another pan ½ oz. butter, add ½ oz. flour and work this
" Roux" till sandy, but do not let it colour. Make up
the mushroom liquor to ½ pint and blend gradually into
the " Roux". Bring to boiling point, then simmer
gently for 10 minutes. Pour in any essence the baked fish
may have exuded. Reduce the sauce if not sufficiently
thick, season, if necessary, and arrange the mushrooms over
the fish. Mask with the sauce, add a delicate dusting of
grated cheese over all, then replace in oven just long
enough to heat well through and glaze the sauce.

Audley End Pudding

2 TABLESPOONS of Cornflour, 1 gill of cream, 2 oz.
butter, 1 pint of milk, a little sugar. Put all this into a
saucepan. Stir over the fire till it boils, let it boil a couple
of minutes or so, but do not let it get thick. Pour into a
shallow fire-proof dish and let it simmer gently 20 minutes
in a coolish oven. The mixture must only be like thick
cream. Just before serving, strew brown sugar on top
and turn it into a crisp caramel under grill.

This pudding is like a glorified cornflour pudding and
most excellent—not necessary to use the cream, but of
course better if it can be got.

From Lady Robertson

Marina Pudding

¼ LB. BUTTER, ¼ lb. castor sugar, 1 lb. chestnuts,
dessertspoonful powdered gelatine, ½ glass sherry, teacup
of double cream, powdered chocolate—whipped cream.

Beat the ¼ lb. fresh butter to a cream, then beat into it
¼ castor sugar and add the lb. of chestnuts, which have
been boiled, skinned and minced in a machine and passed
through a sieve. Mix well and add teacup of cream and
dessertspoon of powdered gelatine, which has been dissolved

in a little warm water. Add the sherry and mix all well together. Turn into a mould and set. Turn out on to a dish for serving, cover with powdered chocolate, then with whipped cream, all over it. Marron glacé can be served with it as a decoration. This pudding can be made with evaporated milk, though of course not so well as with fresh cream.

Apricot Squares

PASTRY, 5 ozs. self-raising flour, 2 ozs. butter, 2 yolks of eggs, pinch of salt, 2 or 3 tablespoons cream or top of milk, 1 lb. apricots (ripe ones).

Work ingredients together on a board. Leave the pastry resting here for 20 minutes, then roll over half of it and place on a greased flat tin.

Cut the apricots in half and stone them, place on the pastry sprinkled well with sugar. Then roll out the other half of the pastry and lay on top. Brush over with sugared milk and bake in the oven 20 to 25 minutes. Cut in squares when cool.

(This is a delicious little dish done by an Austrian Cook.)

From Mrs. Brinsley Ford.

Ham " Southern Style "

SOAK A HAM for 48 hours. In the morning boil in enough water to cover it, to which add 1 pint of white vinegar (allow ¼ hour to each lb.)

Let the ham cool in the water it was boiled in, and when cool, remove the skin, and trim carefully.

Mix 1 cup of brown sugar with 1 beaten egg, so that it is a smooth paste. This is to be spread over the ham (which is now placed in the baking tin) and 1 pint of white vinegar is poured into the tin.

Bake for 1 hour—basting frequently.

This gives it the rich moist taste and flavour of champagne.

Janson's Temptation

A LAYER OF POTATOES (raw), cut in fine needles, is put in a well-buttered fireproof dish, then a layer of filleted (Norwegian) anchovies, and another layer of potatoes. Thick cream is poured on, and the dish is put in a fairly hot oven (½ hour—¾ hour). If one likes, a little chopped onion is nice to add. A nice dish for a *hors-d'oeuvre*.

From Mrs. Swanberg

Prunes or Figs for Grilled Cutlets, etc.

TAKE SOME French plums or figs, about 1¼ lbs., put them in a stewpan with enough claret to cover them, a few drops of carmine, ¼ lb. of red currant jelly, ½ oz. castor sugar. Bring to the boil and then simmer for about ¼ hour; then thicken to the state of cream with a little crême de Riz that has been mixed till smooth with a little strained lemon juice. Stir till boiling, and use.

N.B.—We find figs require much more claret than prunes as they absorb more. We keep on adding it as it reduces, or else they come to the table a bit dry.

From Mrs. Holland Warne

White Rice

MELT SOME BUTTER in a frying-pan. Cook the rice in it about 5 minutes or *less—shaking the pan the whole time*. Strain, put into large saucepan of boiling salted water and cook steadily until soft—strain and rinse with boiling water—then let stand on the stove for a few minutes before serving. A cloth over the colander will help to take the steam.

For Brown Rice

PROCEED IN THE same manner, cooking the rice in the butter until a nut brown.

NOTE.—Do *not* wash rice before cooking it in the butter.   *From Lady Brock*

Ris de Veau Chautraine

TAKE A FINE sweetbread. Let it soak for 3 hours in cold salted water. After that, boil in fresh water with a few peppercorns for 20 minutes.

Then drain well, and put between 2 plates with a weight on top till required.

Then cook the sweetbread in butter for 20 minutes in a casserole over a slow fire. Add a port wine glass of brandy which is to be set alight, and then add 3 times the amount you have of brandy of double (very thick) cream, 3 soupspoons of meat glaze, and the juice of $\frac{1}{4}$ of a lemon, 3 tiny spoonfuls of French mustard, salt and pepper to taste.

Leave this to reduce over a slow fire till the sauce has thickened.

A few croutons fried in butter may be served with the Sweetbread.

From Restaurant Chautraine, Bruxelles, and Mrs. Ralph Barnett

Sweetbreads under Glass

THE SWEETBREADS having been blanched, and all skin and sinew removed, cut into small pieces, put on to well-buttered toast that fits into bottom of your small fireproof saucer. Put a mushroom over and *very little* chopped onion. Pour over this very thick cream and a bit of butter, pepper and salt. Put on a glass cover and stand on stove; keep moving from cool to hot side, filling up the glasses with a little more cream should the toast get dry, but on no account must the toast, when finished, be swimming in cream—only enough to keep all very moist. Take about 20 minutes to cook this, the sweetbreads being cooked in their own steam.

This is a most excellent dish, and looks delightful and original. It must be sent to the table with the covers on.

To blanch the sweetbreads, they must be soaked in salt and water for at least 3 hours, to extract blood and sinew. Wash well and put into boiling water with a few peppercorns and let boil gently for about 15 minutes. Strain and then put between 2 plates with a weight on top to press and drain. *From the Old Sherrys in New York*

Stew of Sweetbread and Mushrooms

HALF A POUND of sweetbread, 2 tablespoons butter, 2 tablespoons flour, ¼ lb. or small tin of mushrooms, milk, salt, sugar.

The sweetbread is soaked in water and afterwards brought to the boil. The water is poured away and fresh salted water added, and the sweetbread is boiled in it for 20 minutes. The skin is removed and the sweetbread is cut up in small pieces. The butter is melted in saucepan, and the flour and milk added and boiled for 10 minutes and constantly stirred. The little mushrooms and the sweetbread are added, and also salt, pepper and a little sugar to taste. If desirable a little wine or brandy can be added. Have ready a flan of puff pastry and fill with the sweetbreads.

This stew can also be made of lobster or crab instead of sweetbread, and can be used, as filling, in pastry shapes, shells, lobster shells and omelettes. *From Mrs. Swanberg*

Snipe Pudding à l'Epicurien

PLUCK, SINGE, and divide in halves 6 fresh snipe. Remove the gizzards; reserve the trails for use as afterwards directed. Season the snipe with cayenne and lemon juice and a sprinkle of salt, and set them aside until wanted.

Next slice up a Portugal onion, and fry it (with a bit of butter) to a light colour. Throw in a good tablespoonful of flour, some chopped mushrooms, parsley, and moisten with ½ pint of wine.

Stir the whole over the fire to boil—for about 10 minutes, then add the trails, and rub this through a hair sieve. Meanwhile, a pudding basin should be lined with a thin crust of suet paste, the snipe and sauce with some scollops of truffles arranged neatly therein, and covered with the paste.

Steam for 1½ hours. Turn out with care and serve, or serve in the pudding basin.

Swiss Cheese

ONE OZ. EACH of butter, flour and cheese, 2 eggs, 1 breakfast cup of milk. Make a soufflé mixture of butter, flour, cheese and milk, then let cool. Add yolks of eggs, one at a time, beating well after each. Whip whites and add. Steam for 20 minutes in a mould or soufflé dish. Turn out to a gratin dish, cover with cream and grated cheese, and brown in the oven for a few minutes.

It is difficult in this receipt to say the exact time it takes to steam, only practice can tell one, as 20 minutes is often not long enough.

Notes

Notes

CHICKEN AND MEAT DISHES

Chicken in Casserole

FOR EIGHT PEOPLE. Take two good chickens and poach the day before required. Cup up into pieces (either with or without the legs. I generally omit the drumsticks). Put pieces of chicken into casserole with layers of mushrooms, cooked first in butter and chopped up—also a few onions also cooked in butter. Make a good velouté sauce. A pound of tomatoes is made into a purée and is mixed into it, and then a good quantity of cream, one pint at least. The sauce is poured over chicken to cover it thickly. The casserole is stood in a tin of hot water and put into the oven for about ½ hour to cook well through. The sauce should be a pale pink colour and like very thick cream. Do not let it get solid. About ½ lb. mushrooms is enough for two chickens.

From Mrs. Holland Warne

Chickens and Pheasants

CHICKENS AND PHEASANTS are much improved by being first stuffed with a good handful of coarse crumbs well mixed with butter or dripping. The crumbs keep the fat in the bird.

The difference to the quality of the flesh is wonderful, and the gravy should be only what the bird was cooked in—the sides of the pan well scraped to get off all the meat juices, and then all put through a fine strainer. A little water may be added, but never stock.

Another way is to stuff with boiled rice and lots of very fat chopped bacon and mushrooms.

I do this with poussins.

Chicken Terrapin

CUT A BOILED and already cooked chicken into squares, add seasoning, sherry, and cream (to taste), also a hard-boiled egg chopped fine. Warm up together till very hot and serve with rice.

Lobster is excellent done in the same way.

Fricassée de Volaille (Cold)

CUT A CHICKEN, about 4 lbs., in nice pieces. Put into a saucepan with cold water and bring to the boil. Then drain in a colander and cool for 5 minutes in water. Put a piece of butter in a stewpan and partly cook the chicken in it. Then pour 2 spoonfuls of flour on it and about a pint or more of good stock, and let it simmer for 20 minutes. Season with salt and paprika. Place the pieces of chicken in a glass dish. Reduce the sauce by half and add ½ pint of fresh cream. Strain the sauce and then pour over the chicken. Place on top pimentoes and mushrooms, shredded and cooked in butter. Let cool for an hour before serving.

Grilled Chicken—with Tartar Sauce

Quantity for 8 people

TAKE 2 ROASTING chickens and partly cook them. Then joint, using only best parts and dip in following mixture: ¼ lb. butter, 3 ozs. flour, juice of 3 lemons, 1 dessertspoon piquante sauce, 1 dessertspoon of tomato sauce, 1 dessert-spoon French or Savora mustard, 3 yolks of eggs, salt and pepper.

Then roll the pieces in brown crumbs.

Grill until Cooked.

Serve tartar sauce separately.   *From Mrs. Cannicott*

Poulet aux Trois Frères

CUT UP A CHICKEN into small pieces. Melt enough butter to cover the bottom of a casserole, *hot*. Add 2 full teaspoons of olive oil. Put in the chicken and cover with 24 *very* small onions, or shallots, carefully prepared, and 30 very small whole new potatoes. Flavour with salt and pepper and a pinch of mace. Add a few mushrooms cut in medium pieces. Put the whole in the oven. It should be well done in 40 minutes and the whole dish a good brown colour. Just before serving, pour over 3 or 4 tablespoonfuls of dissolved meat glaze.

Soufflé de Volaille à l'Indienne

TAKE MEAT from a chicken breast, pound it well, add 2 tablespoonfuls of Béchamel sauce, 2 raw eggs and 1 oz. butter. Pass all through a fine hair sieve, add as much whipped cream as the forcemeat will take, about ½ pint, and the whites of 2 eggs whipped stiff. Take a soufflé dish, put in a layer of Patna rice (cooked), then a layer of rich curry until the dish is half-full of rice and curry sauce. Pour the chicken mixture on top and steam gently for about 40 minutes. Before it is done put the whites of 3 eggs (well-whipped) on top of steamed soufflé and let it remain until the whites are cooked. Serve with boiled rice and curry sauce separately.

From Mrs. Basil Buckley

White Curry Sauce

MAKE A GOOD Béchamel sauce. You have already prepared some for the soufflé, add a little curry powder, and cook well after the curry powder is added; or else a brown curry sauce.

White Devil No. 1

WHIP ½ PINT of cream into a tablespoon of mixed mustard, 1 tablespoon of Harvey or similar sauce and 1 of Worcester sauce and a little pepper and salt.

Pour over chicken or game, which should be already heated through. Bake in a quick oven for 5 minutes. Serve with boiled rice.

N.B.—The game or chicken is already cooked, and boiling fowls are excellent cooked in this way.

White Devil No. 2

SPREAD FRENCH MUSTARD over the pieces of chicken or game, or lamb (all having been already cooked). Put the meat into a small casserole and pour over it the following :

One teaspoonful of French mustard, 1 teaspoonful anchovy sauce, 1 teaspoonful of French vinegar, 1 teasspconful salt, 1 teaspoonful castor sugar, ½ teaspoonful of Harvey sauce, ½ teaspoonful of Worcester sauce.

Mix all these well, and take a teacupful of cream, whip it and add to the mixture. Mix all well together. Pour this over the chicken or game and brown well in the oven.

From Lady Brock

Pigeons en Casserole

TAKE THREE YOUNG pigeons trussed for boiling. Lard each with a strip of fat bacon, fry them in butter till nicely browned, drain them and put them into a casserole with just enough good gravy barely to cover them. Add 3 or 4 little green onions and a few button mushrooms, together with a good glass of claret and a seasoning of salt and

coralline pepper. Let the birds cook very slowly for
¾ hour at the side of fire, and then when cooked serve up
in same casserole.

American Stuffing

TWO CUPS coarse-grated breadcrumbs. Season with
onion juice, salt and pepper, chopped parsley and a little
grated rind of lemon and a little thyme.

Put 2 good tablespoonfuls of butter into a saucepan.
When melted (not allowed to brown) throw in your
seasoning and breadcrumbs with a large fork. Turn lightly
and quickly, then put into your fowl.

The stuffing should be light as a feather.

From Mrs. Buckley

Braised Beef in Jelly

LARD A NEATLY rolled sirloin of beef weighing between
5 or 6 lbs. with strips of fat bacon and truffles, and insert
little pieces of the bacon and truffle round the sides of the
meat as well as on the top. Then put it into a braising pan,
which has been spread with 1 oz. of beef dripping and
prepared with a thick layer of sliced vegetables (onion,
carrot, and turnip) and let it fry for 20 minutes. Then add
a blade of mace, 2 cloves, 12 whole black peppers, ½ small
teaspoonful of salt, a little touch of parsley and herbs, and
a pint of brown stock. Cover the meat closely with a
buttered paper, then put on the lid of the pan and cook
it in a moderately hot oven for 3 hours. Turn out the meat
after it has been in the oven 1½ hours, and baste it from
time to time. When it is done, remove it from the pan and
press it between two flat dishes until it is cold. Line a
round tin, which is sufficiently large to take the meat, with
a thick coating of nicely flavoured aspic jelly, which should
be of a deep golden colour, and when the beef is cold,

wipe it and trim it and put it into the prepared tin and pour in sufficient cool aspic entirely to cover it. The following day dip the mould quickly into hot water and then turn out the beef. Surround it by chopped golden aspic jelly and garnish here and there with little bunches of watercress. The top of the meat may be ornamented with leaf-shaped pieces of the red jelly.

Pressed Brisket of Beef

TAKE A LEAN piece of salt brisket, about 5 or 6 lbs. weight, having had the bones removed.

Mix together a teaspoonful of ground mace, a teaspoonful of black pepper, a teaspoonful of ground cloves and a saltspoonful of grated nutmeg. Rub the under portion of the meat well with the spices, then skewer it into shape and tie it tightly in a piece of pudding-cloth. Put it into a saucepan containing sufficient tepid water to cover the meat. Bring the water gradually to boiling point, then put in 2 medium-sized onions (each stuck with 3 cloves), a carrot, a thick slice of fat bacon and the bones from the meat. Cover the saucepan closely and let the meat simmer steadily for as many hours as there are pounds of meat (weighed after the bones are out), adding more water from time to time as that in the pan evaporates. When done, leave the beef in the cloth and place it under a weight until the following day. Then remove the cloth, and to make the meat look specially good pour some warm aspic jelly over and put to set in a cool place.

12th Lancer Ham

PUT A HAM of about 12 lbs. to soak in cold water for about 24 hours. Then boil for 2 hours. Skin it and stick it all over with cloves, about 1 in. apart. Put in a baking-tin and put in the oven, basting with 1 pint stout, to which add 10 ozs. Demerara sugar. Baste until the stout and sngar make a thick glaze, which should be in about ½ hour.

Boiled Suet Pudding of Lamb and Oysters

TAKE THE MEAT from the neck of lamb, cut in smallish pieces, not too thin. Roll in flour seasoned with pepper and salt and lay in a basin you have lined with a good suet crust. Now add a little finely chopped onion and half a dozen chopped oysters. Pour in a little stock so that the pudding will be nice and moist, and cover with suet paste. The pudding must be boiled in a floured cloth for 2½ to 3 hours. A very good dish.

To Braise Neck of Lamb

PUT INTO A braising pan a good pat of butter, some vegetables, carrots and leeks, and on them lay the best end neck of lamb, with the chump end left on, so that it stands up nicely when carved. Put it with the fat side down and put on fire to fry until the meat is a golden brown on both sides. Then add a little consommé or good stock, just enough to cover the vegetables, and having covered the pan simmer very slowly. When half-cooked, remove pan to oven and finish braising the meat there without a cover. Let the meat cool in the braising pan and when cold put it on the dish it is to be served in and pour over a very strong meat jelly, made of course without gelatine, and let set. If the jelly is nice and clear, the joint looks almost better without any garnishing, especially if served in a deep brown fireproof dish.

Such a good receipt for a lunch party on a very hot day.

Lamb and Sprue

TAKE A NECK or breast of lamb, and lay it in a saucepan

on to a good bunch of sprue, cut in pieces about 3 inches long, a small head of celery cut small, one onion, pepper and salt and a sprig of parsley. Put only enough water or light stock just to cover the meat, and simmer very gently till the meat and sprue are tender. A couple of small lumps of sugar improve the flavour. Be careful there is not too much liquor, and all the fat should be removed. The sprue should surround the meat when served and also be thickly laid over it.

Noisettes of Lamb

MAKE 8 OR 10 NOISETTES from a small loin of lamb, or best end. Cut them small but thick. Either grill, or else egg and breadcrumb and fry. Arrange them down the side of a fireproof dish, with on one side a very good purée of mashed potato, and serve in sauce boat a *sauce Maltaise*, made as follows :

Make a good velouté sauce and add some finely chopped parsley, shallots and mushrooms. Dilute it with a little sherry, and a squeeze or so of orange juice and some finely shredded orange rind.

To make your *velouté sauce* :

Put in saucepan a piece of butter the size of an egg. Add the same quantity of flour. Cook one minute and add very slowly some veal or chicken stock. Bring up to the boil, whipping all the time. Season with salt and pepper, a pinch of nutmeg and a little parsley and mushroom stalks. Let this simmer and thicken, and pass through a strainer.

Veal with Cream

TAKE ABOUT 1 or 2 lbs. veal cutlet, cut up in small pieces about 1½ inches long, cover them lightly with paprika pepper and salt, and fry for a few seconds. Then place in a casserole with some rashers of bacon—streaky

and cut very thin—a small quantity of Spanish onion, which
has been chopped very fine and fried in butter till a nice
gold colour, and a small piece of butter, and cook all this
in a moderately hot oven for just over 2 hours, watching
that the veal does not get dry (in which case add a little
more butter). When it is cooked, strain off a small
quantity of the gravy, and pour some cream, about ½ pint,
to cover the veal. Be careful that your oven is not too
hot or your cream will curdle.   *From Sophy, Lady Hall*

Veal Pudding or Gâteau de Veau

ABOUT 2 TO 2¼ LBS. veal cutlet is wanted to produce
1½ lbs. after going through the mincing machine.

Pass through sausage machine enough of veal cutlet to
make 1½ lbs. weight—see that no sinews remain—put
this meat into a big basin and add 6 oz. chopped beef suet,
5 ozs. chopped tongue, 3 ozs. butter, 3 tablespoons breadcrumbs, 4 or 5 tablespoons cream, 6 tablespoons gravy,
or water with Liebig (latter is best), 1 tablespoon lemon
juice, 2 yolks and 1 white (beat up together), about 1 good
teaspoon salt and one small teaspoon pepper. Now it is
best to knead all this together well and lightly with the
hand, as if mixing a cake—let it cool in the larder—after
mixing—have a proper sized tin and put lots of butter
on it all over the tin—next take the whole lump of meat
and shape it with the hand into a long round roll like a
huge sausage, place it on butter on tin and bake it in a hot
oven for quite an hour, *basting it constantly* or else it dries.
To make it look frothy, at last moment sprinkle a little
flour and just hold it in front of fire before dishing it. For
gravy, add a few tablespoons water to the butter, etc., in
tin *after* pudding is taken up.   *Swedish receipt*

Escalopes de Veau Brownie

TAKE SOME veal cutlet, about 1½ lbs., cut as thin as

possible and in rounds about the size of the palm of one's hand. Beat the meat well (this should always be done to veal escalopes) to flatten and shape them. Season with salt and pepper. Heat your sauté pan, and when hot put in a piece of butter, and when at the foaming point lay in the veal, flat and not on top of one another. Cook for about 5 minutes, shaking pan to keep the frying even. Then take about ½ lb. mushrooms, cut in long strips that have already been well cooked in butter. Stir them in and go on frying after this. A good tablespoon of finely chopped parsley is then scattered over the veal, which has now been cooking 8 to 10 minutes. Take off fire and throw in a small wineglass of brandy, return to fire and let the brandy flare up. Take off fire until the flame dies down, and then add a good drop of cream. A small cupful should be enough for 4 to 6 people. Stir all up well for a few seconds more over the fire and the veal is ready.

This is a dish which was served to me at Quaglinos, and I can thoroughly recommend it.

Selle de Veau Gratinée

THIS IS A very important dish and perhaps rather complicated, but I have described it as simply as possible, so that I think any cook could manage it, and it is worth trying.

Take the saddle of veal and braise it as follows :

First having browned it in butter all over, lay the saddle in a large sauté pan on a bed of thickly sliced and fried carrots and onions, a Bouquet garni and a little blanched fresh bacon rind. Moisten all with a little good veal stock. Set to boil on a moderate fire and reduce the veal stock with the lid on. When the stock has become a thick glaze, add more fresh stock and reduce as before. The third time moisten the veal until it is half-covered and put the pan into a moderate oven. The meat must be constantly basted while it cooks, in order to prevent it drying. Braised white meat must on no account be over-cooked, or it is dry and spoilt. You can tell when it is done by sticking a braiding needle into the joint, and if an absolutely colourless liquid exudes it is ready. Now, having braised your saddle, let it get partly cold. Take a small sharp knife and draw a line within ½ inch of the extreme edge on either side and end, pressing the knife along the meat in so doing. Proceed in the same way on either side of the chine and remove the fillets from the joint, severing them very carefully. The saddle now forms on each side a case, and into this cavity you pour a thick purée of mushrooms and cream. Now cut your fillets into escallops, not too thin, and return them to their places in the joint, arranging them in such a way as to make them then appear untouched. Lay on each some more mushrooms, cooked, and some pieces of truffle. As soon as the saddle is reconstructed cover all with a rich Béchamel sauce. Powder all well with Parmesan cheese and put into oven to reheat and glaze. Strain the braising gravy well and serve in a sauce bowl, also another bowl of the purée of mushrooms.

Given by the Chef of the Duc de Doudeauville

to Mr. Arthur Heathfield

Notes

Notes

Notes

VEGETABLES

Beetroot au Gratin

BOIL 4 BEETROOTS and when cold cut into cubes or slices. Slightly butter a round soufflé dish and sprinkle with grated cheese. Put in the cut-up beetroot and add sufficient cream nearly to fill the dish, some more grated cheese and some small lumps of butter on top. Bake until lightly browned in the oven for about 10 minutes.

From Mrs. Walter Brinton

Timbale of Chou-fleur

BOIL A CAULIFLOWER till tender but still firm. Take and break into branches and put these on a cloth to drain. Butter a plain round mould and sprinkle it well with brown crumbs. Put ½ pint of milk into a stewpan with a cut-up shallot, a few peppercorns and a blade of mace. Let it boil and then strain, and then add ½ oz. of arrowroot, that you have mixed quite smoothly with 1 oz. of butter. Stir till boiling, then let simmer for a few moments, remove from fire and leave till nearly cool. Then add 2 eggs, season with salt and put a layer of this mixture into the mould. On it sprigs of the cauliflower, and so on until the mould is filled. Stand the mould in a sauté pan and pour round a little boiling water, cover with a *well* buttered paper and cook in a moderately hot oven for about 1 hour. Either turn out on a hot dish, or serve in the mould.

A Dish of Leeks

TAKE SOME LEEKS and cut them length required, leaving very little green on them. Parboil them for about 20 minutes and drain well. Place grated cheese in a *buttered* fireproof dish and then a layer of leeks, then again cheese and season to taste. Pour some cream over the leeks and sprinkle some more cheese. Bake in oven until a golden brown and serve very hot.

Spinach Chartreuse

TAKE 1 LB. *cooked* spinach and pass it through a sieve, then whip it into a little more than ¼ pint of liquid aspic jelly. Turn this into a round buttered mould. Put a tumbler into the middle. When set, remove the tumbler. It if sticks, pour a little hot water into it when it will come out easily, and fill up the centre with mayonnaise sauce mixed with a little aspic and some pieces of hard-boiled egg. When all is set, turn out. Place finely chopped aspic on top and some around base with sprigs of parsley or chervil.

Iced Tomatoes and Horseradish Sauce

VERY GOOD TO serve as a salad on a hot summer day are large tomatoes, skinned and put in the ice-chest till very cold, and at last moment some good creamy horse-radish sauce poured over them. The sauce to be just slightly iced. With a joint of cold lamb this is excellent. The best horseradish sauce to use is made by grating some horseradish into a mayonnaise sauce to which has been added some cream : say 3 tablespoons of mayonnaise, gill of cream whipped and 1 tablespoon grated horseradish.

Macédoine of Winter Vegetables

TAKE 3 LARGE carrots, scrape and divide them into 4, lengthwise. Remove all the hard pith and slice them finely. Treat 2 medium-size turnips in the same way. Remove the hard outer skin of a large Spanish onion. Slice it. Put the vegetables into salted, boiling water, together with a little chopped celery. Boil for 20 minutes, carefully removing any scum that rises. Take them out and drain very thoroughly. Put 2 ozs. of butter into a pan, add the vegetables, season them and add a very small lump of sugar. Put a piece of greased paper over the pan and then put on lid. Simmer as gently as possible for about an hour, shaking the pan occasionally. Sprinkle the vegetables with finely chopped parsley. There must be no suggestion of frying in this way of cooking, nor should the vegetables be at all *greasy*. They must not be coloured. If they are simmered gently enough, the butter will keep its freshness. This is essential to the delicacy of the dish. The quantities given are for three persons.

Notes

PUDDINGS AND CREAMS
Apples à la Suédoise

MAKE A SYRUP of ¼ lb. sugar and ½ pint water—add
grated rind of 1 very large or 2 small lemons—peel,
halve and core 6 *medium*-sized dessert apples—put in as
many halves as can lie *beside* each other in the stewpan—
put the lid on—*look*, after 3 minutes, turn them, watch
them well and try with a fork. If they feel soft—then
take them out, and put them in the dish—go on till all are
cooked. Then, if necessary, reduce the syrup, or add a little
lemon-juice if too luscious. Sometimes the apples are dry,
and then a drop of water may have to be added, when
putting the last lot of apples in stewpan. Pour the syrup
over apples on dish and let stand till next day when they
ought to look somewhat like jelly, or rather the syrup
ought to look *set*.

Baked Bananas

PLACE THE skinned bananas in a baking-pan, and on them
put several large pieces of butter. Then add a liberal amount
of granulated sugar.

Squeeze a lemon over the whole, and bake until the
bananas are a nice golden brown colour.

Mix a little powdered cinnamon with some granulated
sugar and serve separately.

An American receipt

Danish Apple Pudding

STEW 3 LBS. OF apples to quite a pulp, leave it to get
cold, then make the following mixture :—¼ lb. ground
almonds, ¼ lb. castor sugar, ¼ lb. butter, yolks of 2 eggs;
mix this to a paste. Put the apple purée at the bottom of a

fireproof dish and spread the paste over it. Bake about ¾ hour a golden brown and the top crisp. Serve with big lumps of whipped cream flavoured with almond or vanilla on top of pudding. Serve quickly so that the cream does not melt—or, even better, serve cold.

Bombe Philadelphia

PUT 2 TABLESPOONSFUL of arrowroot into a basin and mix with ½ pint of cold milk so as to form a smooth paste. Add a pint of hot milk and 8 ozs, of castor sugar. Let it get quite cool and then add ½ pint of cream. Freeze in the usual way, and, when half-frozen, add ½ pint of slightly whipped cream.

Fine Calves-foot Jelly

CUT 4 CALVES FEET, that have been well-soaked and blanched, into small pieces. Put these into a casserole with 3 quarts of water. Cover, and let this boil very slowly, until the liquid is reduced to 1½ quarts. Then pass all through a tammy and let it cool. Then with a knife remove all the grease that is on top and replace in casserole to melt, adding 1 pint of madeira, the juice of 5 lemons and grated peel of 1, sugar to taste. Take the whites of 6 eggs, beat these *with* the shells until it is all beaten to a cream. Add this mousse to the rest and boil all together 20 minutes. Then pass all through a jelly bag, and do this several times until the jelly is absolutely clear.

An old French receipt

Charlotte Chantilly

FILL THE SIDES of a charlotte mould with biscuits (called in France 'Biscuits à la Cuillère') which are thin crisp sponge fingers.

Fill the middle of the mould with well-beaten cream

to which is added 2 whites of egg, beaten very stiff. Cover the top of the mould with more of the biscuits, and then put on ice for 3 hours.

At the last minute turn out the cream, and put around it a *rich* syrup of raspberries or strawberries, flavoured with Kirsche. *From Mr. Ballard-Smith, Dinard*

Crème Brùlé

BOIL ½ PINT CREAM for one minute, pour it on the yolks of 2 very fresh eggs, well-beaten. Put on the fire and let it just come to the boil, then pour into a soufflé case. Put in a slow oven for 10 minutes, taking great care not to let it boil. Serve cold with a little caramel syrup on top. To make this cream well, it must be watched all the time it is in the oven, for if the mixture once boils it is spoilt and becomes too rich and sticky.

Crème Sibella

THREE YOLKS of eggs—2 tablespoons of castor sugar. Beat well together in Bain Marie (put your basin of eggs, etc., in saucepan of hot water). Then stir in 2 sheets of gelatine (well dissolved in 2 tablespoons of milk first)— and add ¼ pint of whipped cream. Then the whipped whites of the eggs. Pour into low glass dish with a liquid caramel sauce over.

You boil your water until very hot and put your basin to balance on top, not in the water, as it would make the cream too hot. You do this on the kitchen table after you have heated your water.

From Miss Sybel Williams

Crème Fruits

ONE QUART of milk, ¼ lb. of sugar, ¼ lb. of flour, 3 yolks

and 3 whole eggs, 4 leaves of gelatine, chopped dice of crystallized fruit, grated lemon.

Mix the sugar, flour, yolks of whole eggs, and grate of lemon all together, add gradually the boiling milk and the gelatine, previously soaked. Stir until it boils, and add dice of fruits which have been sprinkled with liqueur.

Pour out and allow to cool on tin.

Cut into square pieces about an inch thick. Egg and crumb and fry in clarified butter.

Serve with an apricot sauce, flavoured with liqueur.

Grease the tin or marble slab before turning out the mixture, or it will stick.

Cup Puddings

BEAT 2 OZS. BUTTER and 2 ozs. castor sugar to a cream. Add 1 egg (a large one) well-beaten to the mixture. Flavour with a few drops of lemon juice and stir in gradually just under 3 ozs. flour. Bake in a hot oven in little buttered moulds and put a paper over them to keep them from burning brown. These little puddings made from this receipt are very soft and light.

Délice de Chocolat

MILK, ½ LB. chocolate, add 2 tablespoonfuls of brandy and 4 yolks of eggs. Mix all this well. Now beat up stiffly the whites of 4 eggs and stir in. Place in a mould and stand on ice 10 hours before using. Serve with stewed fruit; a compote of plums goes best. The chocolate must be soft when finished.

From Mrs. Thorpe

Fruit Mould

ONE QUART OF fresh currant juice or 1 pint syrup and

1 pint water, 1 oz. cornflour, and sugar to taste. Mix the syrup and cornflour well before putting on the fire and then boil for 8 or 10 minutes and turn out and let get cold. Serve with whipped cream or custard.

Fruit Salad in Jelly

MAKE AN ORDINARY wine jelly, but with a mixture of rum and maraschino, and even sometimes a little sherry, or any thing that is going. The jelly is then broken up in pieces and added to the fruit salad, and is a great improvement to the ordinary salad.

A sponge or madeira cake that has become dry is excellent cut in small thickish slices and toasted in oven till very crisp, to serve with fruit or ices.

Another very good Fruit Salad

DIVIDE 3 ORANGES into sections and remove all pips and pith. Skin and seed ½ lb. of grapes. Cut into halves 1 lb. of strawberries. Blanch ¼ lb. of almonds and cut into strips. Cut into small chunks 1 or 2 slices of pineapple.

Mix these fruits together and moisten them with lemon juice and maraschino in the proportion of 1 wineglassful of maraschino to 3 of the lemon juice. The lemon juice should be sweetened before the liqueur is put in.

Put in glass dish or large wine glasses, and let it stand on ice until very cold.

A few glacé cherries or crystallised violets can be sprinkled on top.

Grape-fruit Macédoine

MIX THE GRAPE-FRUIT cut in pieces with some fresh fruit, strawberries, raspberries, or else some tinned fruit. Add a little rum or sherry.

Fill the glasses with the fruit, and on top put some

pieces of preserved ginger, or marron glacé, or any candied fruit soaked in wine.

Stand on ice until very cold, and serve with some biscuits or cake.

Grape-fruit Suprême

CUT UP HALF A grape-fruit. Add ½ tablespoon of sherry, ½ tablespoon of cream and small teaspoonful of sugar. Well mix together and pour over fruit. Put on ice till very cold.

Glacé à la Grappe de Muscat

PREPARE I PINT of cornflour to the consistency of cream, add sugar to taste. When cool, mix 1 pint of slightly whipped cream and a little brandy. Put into a freezing machine and turn until it is frozen all through, then pack it into a bombé mould for 2 or 3 hours; and before serving, scoop out the centre and fill up with grapes that have been skinned and soaked in brandy.

A Simple Ice-cream

MAKE A PINT of rich custard by adding 4 yolks of eggs to 1 pint of milk. Put on fire in a double-boiler, stirring constantly until the custard thickens and coats the spoon. Add some caramel (which you have made by putting 3 tablespoons of powdered sugar with 2 of water into a saucepan. Stir the sugar till melted and let it get a golden colour). Allow this to get nearly cold and then stir in 2 whites of eggs beaten very stiff, and ½ teaspoon of vanilla flavouring. When all is cold, add 1 pint of thick cream and freeze. Enough for 6 people.

Macaroon Ice-cream

ONE QUART OF cream, 6 ozs. sugar, 1 tablespoonful of vanilla essence, macaroons, blanched almonds, preserved chestnuts.

Pound 1 lb. of macaroons, which add to the cream beaten stiff, then the vanilla essence and the sugar.

Beat all together and freeze.

Serve in glasses with whipped cream sweetened and flavoured with a drop of almond essence. Decorate with the almonds cut into shreds, and put a glacé marron on top of each glass.

Marlborough Tart

LINE A FLAT TIN (like for a flan) with puff pastry. Take 2 ozs. of mixed peel chopped very small and sprinkle over the pastry. Mix 6 ozs. of butter, 6 ozs. of brown sugar and the yolks of 4 eggs. Put the mixture in a stewpan, boil for 1 minute, then pour it over the pastry. Bake for about ½ hour. Can be served hot or cold.

From Mrs. Pirie

Mincemeat

ONE POUND OF apples peeled and chopped fine, 1 lb. of suet, 1 lb. of brown sugar, 1 gill of brandy, 1 gill of white wine, 2 nutmegs, some powdered cinnamon, 1 lb. of currants washed and dried, 1 lb. of raisins stoned, 6 ozs. of mixed peel, salt to taste.

Mix well together and put into a crock, cover with bladder. This ought to be made in November for Christmas.

Orange Jelly

LEAF GELATINE ½ oz., 1 gill water, ¼ lb. loaf sugar, 4 oranges, 1 lemon, ½ gill sherry.

First wash the oranges and dry them. Peel one very thinly and steep the peel in the wine for 1 hour. Then soak the gelatine in half the water, stir over the fire until dissolved, strain on to ¼ lb. sugar, add ¼ gill hot water. When sugar is melted, stir the juice and pulp of oranges and juice of lemon; add sherry, taking out peel. Put into a moistened mould and leave it in a cool place to set.

Old-fashioned. *From Miss Savile*

Parfait au Thé

PUT 6 EGG YOLKS into a basin, add to them ½ pint of syrup and whisk over hot water until the consistency of cream. Take the basin off the hot water and add 1 gill of tea, which should be freshly made and fairly strong. Let the mixture cool, then whip ½ pint of cream and stir into preparation. Pour into a prepared mould and bury it in ice and salt for 4 hours.

Peaches Zabbaglione

A change from the ordinary Zabbaglione

PUT INTO A shallow dish some peaches cut in half (if tinned cook them a little first) and over them put some small strawberries with a little sweetened syrup. Make some *Zabbaglione* as follows :—

Beat thoroughly together 3 yolks of eggs and 5 ozs. of castor sugar, add a little grated lemon peel and put into a double saucepan on a very slow fire, or by the side. Beat continually and add by degrees a glass of either marsala or sherry, go on with the beating until the mixture thickens and becomes very frothy. Then pour over the peaches and serve at once.

From Miss Sybel Williams

Pineapple for Dessert

IF THIS IS CUT in slices some hours before serving, and powdered with sugar to taste, and then lemon juice is poured over and between the slices, a good quantity, the pine is a much better flavour, besides removing all the acidity. It is almost better after 24 hours.

Iced Pineapple and Cranberry Sauce

CUT SOME SLICES of fresh pineapple fairly thick and let them soak in a thick syrup flavoured with brandy for some hours. Freeze in the ice machine some clotted cream or, if not at hand, fresh dairy cream. When nearly frozen, add some chopped glacé cherries and return to the freezer to harden. Make a sauce of fresh cranberries, add the syrup of sugar from the pine and cook till soft. Then strain and set aside to cool. When ready, turn out the ice-cream on to the slices of pineapple and serve the cranberry sauce with them.

Pistachio Parfait

HALF POUND OF SUGAR, ⅓ gill of water, whites of 3 eggs, 1 tablespoonful of vanilla essence, 1 teaspoonful of almond essence, 1 pint of cream, a few drops of green colour, 1 gill of chopped pistachio nuts. Boil the sugar and water together until the syrup will thread when dropped from the tip of a spoon. Pour slowly, while beating constantly, on to the whites of eggs beaten until stiff, and continue the beating until the mixture is stiff. Colour the cream a delicate green, and beat until stiff. Combine the mixtures, add the essences and nut meats and freeze, using 3 parts of finely crushed ice to 1 part of salt. Mould and pack in ice and salt.

Remove from the mould, and surround with whipped cream, sweetened and flavoured with vanilla essence. Sprinkle with chopped pistachio nuts.

Poires Durand

FIRST MAKE A good rich round Genoese cake, the size to depend on the number of pears you require to stand on it. The cake need not be more than 1½ inches high. Poach the pears you require, one for each person, in slightly sweetened syrup and let get cold. Then roll them in some good vanilla-flavoured powdered chocolate. Whip some double cream, enough to make a thick head over the cake, at least 2 inches high. Do not whip cream too stiff. Into this stick your chocolate pears, standing up, the stalk end upwards. The pears must be the best dessert pears, and the larger they are the more effective the dish. A little brandy or liqueur can be sprinkled over the cake before the cream is poured on. This is an exceedingly pretty dish, and I first saw it years ago at the Restaurant Durand in Paris.

Raspberry Compote

FOR A RASPBERRY compote the fresh fruit should never be cooked. Put the raspberries into a bowl, keeping back enough to put through a sieve. The juice from these is then poured over the fruit in bowl, having been sweetened to taste, and put on ice till required. The colour and flavour of the raspberries, done like this, are quite different from cooked fruit.

Rice Pudding

THIS IS SO SELDOM well made, as it takes a long time and a good deal of trouble, but if the pudding is made in the following way, one is well rewarded. This receipt I copied from a paper many years ago, and have never seen this method of making rice pudding in any cookery book since.

Put 2 or 3 large spoonfuls of rice into a buttered pudding

basin, fill with milk. Put into a quick oven about 9.30 a.m. if wanted for lunch. Stir in the cream that forms on top every 5 minutes, not allowing any skin to form.

After stirring 1 hour put a few scraps of butter, or better still, suet over the top, and let skin form.

Remove to cool oven undisturbed for 4 hours.

This pudding is as if made of thick cream.

French Rice Pudding

THIS PUDDING used to be made for me years ago by a cook in France. I think it must have been her own idea, as I have never come across it again. It is very good and simple :

Take 2 tablespoons of rice, put them in a double boiler with about a pint of milk and flavour with lemon peel. Simmer very slowly, and when the rice has used up all the milk add a little more if necessary. When the rice is cooked and the grains well-swelled, take off the fire and let it stand till cool, or till wanted. Beat up the whites of 2 eggs to a very stiff froth. Stir these lightly into the rice and pour into a shallow fireproof or Pyrex glass dish and bake in oven about 15 minutes, but this depends upon heat, etc.; just watch that the pudding is brown on top and the whites and rice just creamy, not stiff.

Soufflé Rice Pudding

ONE OUNCE Carolina rice, 1 egg, ½ pint milk, 1 teaspoon sugar. Simmer the rice, sugar and milk in a double saucepan until cooked. Let cool and then beat in the yolk of the egg, finally the stiffly beaten white. Put in a buttered soufflé dish and brown in the oven.

Russian Cream

BEAT 3 YOLKS very creamy with about 4 ozs. of castor

sugar (½ hour). Add some *very strong* black coffee (2-3 small spoonfuls).

Whip pint of cream stiffly, mix with egg cream and put on the ice. *From Lady Brock*

Cream of Sago

THREE TABLESPOONFULS of fine sago put into a double cooker with ¾ pint of milk. Boil 2 hours, sweeten and flavour with lemon or vanilla. When cold thin down with milk and cream.

Better made the day before use.

Soufflé Praliné au Chocolat

THREE EGGS, 1 oz. castor sugar, ¼ oz. gelatine, 2 ozs. almond rock, ½ gill cream, ½ oz. chocolate, juice of half a lemon, 1 dessertspoon curacoa, a little vanilla flavouring.

Whisk the yolks of eggs with the sugar over hot water until it resembles thick cream. Dissolve the gelatine in a little water, and the chocolate in milk, and strain both mixtures. Pound the almond rock and add. Also stir in the liqueur and a few drops of vanilla, and the lemon juice. Whisk up last of all the white of eggs that have been whisked to a stiff froth. Pour into a soufflé mould, and scatter chopped pistachio nuts on top. Serve in the soufflé dish and put into refrigerator for an hour or two. The almond rock should taste like little gritty bits in the cream; it gives texture and takes off the mawkishness of chocolate. It is inclined to disappear in the soufflé. Perhaps the best way is not to pound too small and to drop into the mixture just before it sets. *From Lady Robertson*

Cold Soufflé

MAKE A RICH custard with 3 yolks of eggs, ½ pint milk

and a little cream, 1 dessertspoonful sugar and a couple of drops of vanilla essence, or any flavouring preferred. Add ¼ oz. of gelatine, which has been soaked in cold water, mix well with the custard and when nearly set add the 3 whites of eggs whipped very stiffly. Pour into a charlotte mould and leave in cold place to set, then turn out and pour thick cream all over. This pudding is very good served with a fruit compote.

Simple Tapioca Soufflé

BOIL SMALL SAUCEPAN of milk with some sugar and lemon peel for flavouring. When boiling, put in about 4 dessertspoonfuls of fine French tapioca. Keep stirring all the time to prevent getting lumpy. When well cooked and thick, take off fire. Beat up 3 yolks of eggs in a basin and by degrees add to the hot mixture, very carefully, so as to prevent the eggs getting into lumps. Leave to cool, and about ¼ hour before serving beat 3 or more whites of eggs to a very stiff froth and mix with the tapioca. Put some powdered sugar on top. Put in fairly cool oven to rise; will take about ¼ hour, but it depends on the oven.

Velvet Cream

PUT 1 OZ. OF GELATINE into ¼ pint of white wine the night before it is to be used; in the morning put it on the fire to dissolve, let it simmer slowly until it does; then strain it into a large bowl with sugar to taste, the juice of 2 large lemons, and then pour on to these ingredients 1 pint of rich cream. Beat this until very thick; it takes about ½ to ¾ hour to beat it.

An old Boston (U.S.A.) receipt from Mr. Arthur Heathfield

Notes

CAKES AND BISCUITS
Almond and Barley Cake

SIX OUNCES ICING sugar (we use honey), 4 ozs. butter, 5 eggs, 4 ozs. Robinson's patent barley, 6 ozs. ground almonds. Cream the butter and add the sugar, work together for 10 minutes and add 1 wineglass of rosewater. Mix ground almonds and barley together, then mix 1 tablespoon of this with the butter and sugar, add 1 egg and beat the mixture again; continue adding dry ingredients alternately with eggs until all is in, then add 1 teaspoon carmine and 1 teaspoonful baking powder. Brush a mould or tin well with warm butter or lard, then dust it over with crème de riz and sugar mixed in equal quantities, then put cake in. Bake in a moderately hot oven for 1 hour and then take from the mould. When cold cut the cake in 2 or 3 slices, put a thick layer of almond butter icing between each slice and close up cake in original form. Colour the remaining almond butter pink and decorate outside of cake.

Almond Butter Icing

WORK ¼ LB. BUTTER to a cream, add 6 oz. icing sugar (or honey) and work well together, then add ¼ lb. ground almonds, 2 tablespoons rosewater, 3 drops almond essence and use as instructed.

Australian Tea Cake

TWO CUPS OF FLOUR, ¼ cup of sugar, 1 cup of milk, 2 eggs, 3 teaspoonfuls of baking powder, a little salt. Mix flour, baking powder, salt and sugar together; beat the eggs, add milk to eggs, beat into flour. Bake in very hot oven for 10 or 15 minutes. Split with sharp knife and butter well while hot.

This is the *most* delicious tea cake.

From Miss La Primaudaye

Irish Bread

ONE POUND OF flour, 1 small teaspoonful of carbonate of soda, 1 pint of thick buttermilk or sour milk, a pinch of salt.

Mix the dry ingredients together, and work the buttermilk in. Bake from 25 minutes to ½ hour in a slow oven.

From Miss Ruth Anderson

Salt Bread Biscuits I

ONE POUND OF flour, a little salt, 1½ ozs. of butter mixed with milk and tepid water.

Roll out thin, prick, cut and bake.

Salt Bread Biscuits II

ONE POUND OF flour, a little salt, 1½ ozs. of butter.

Melt the butter in the water, and add a little milk. Mix up into a dry paste, then roll out on a floured slab into a very thin wafer-like paste. Do not prick.

Cut this out into large rounds the size of pudding plates, and put on slightly floured tins. Bake in a moderate oven until a pale colour and crisp.

Brown Loaf

HALF POUND wholemeal flour, ¼ lb. white flour, ½ teaspoon carbonate of soda, 1 teaspoon of salt, ¼ teaspoon cream of tartar, lump of butter size of walnut.

Mix slowly with a little milk to a stiff dough—flour a flat tin and bake ¾ hour.

Brown Scones

HALF POUND brown flour, 1 egg, 2 ozs. butter, 1 dessert-spoon baking powder, milk, salt.

Put flour, baking powder and ½ teaspoon of salt in basin. Mix all well together. Rub in butter. Beat the egg up with sufficient milk to make a soft dough. Roll out and cut into rounds, or whatever shape liked. Bake in moderate oven for 15 to 20 minutes. Brown scones always take longer to bake than white.

Cherry Cake

BEAT ½ LB. OF butter with ½ lb. castor sugar to a cream. Add by degrees 6 yolks of eggs, well beaten, then 1 cup of milk. Take 1 lb. fine flour. Put into it 1 lb. glacé cherries and 2 teaspoonfuls of cream of tartar. Add the flour, etc., to the mixture, beating all the time. Have the 6 whites of the eggs whisked to a stiff froth, add by degrees to the flour. Finally, a teaspoonful of carbonate of soda mixed in a little milk is to be added. Pour into a greased mould and bake at first in quick oven to rise, after that finish in a cooler one. Putting the glacé cherries into the dry flour prevents them all falling to the bottom of cake when baked.

Chocolate Sponge Cake

FOUR EGGS, 6 ozs. of sugar, 4 ozs. chocolate, 3 ozs. flour, ¼ teaspoon baking powder. Separate yolks from whites, add sugar to yolks with 2 tablespoons of cold water, and beat over hot water till thick and creamy. Meanwhile have the chocolate melted in 4 tablespoons of water, add it to the yolks mixture, add flour and baking powder. Now beat the whites to a stiff froth, mix whites and mixture very lightly together, pour into two *well greased* sandwich tins and bake in a moderate oven for ½ hour. Cream some

butter and icing sugar, put between the sponge, dust
with icing sugar.   *From Lady Brock*

Club Biscuits

ONE POUND flour, 4 ozs. butter, 1 pinch salt. Add water
to make the dough consistent. Then roll it very thin and
cut out size required. To be cooked in a very hot oven.
Do not let them burn.   *From Mrs. Engleheart*

Doboz Torte

THREE AND A HALF OZS. flour, 3½ ozs. castor sugar,
3½ ozs. butter, 4 eggs, ½ lb. plain flavoured chocolate.

Whip sugar and eggs over hot water till creamy, add the
flour, and lastly the butter, melted, but not oiled. Spread
out on baking sheet in very thin rounds about the size of
a pudding plate, about 6 or 8 rounds. The rounds take
about 10 minutes to cook in a medium oven be careful not
to over cook or they will break easily. Sandwich the
rounds with the chocolate butter cream and pour the
caramel over the top round and spread the cream round the
sides which are then covered with grated chocolate.

The butter cream is made with 2 ozs. lump sugar boiled,
to the thread. Pour on 2 yolks of eggs and whip till thick—
cool and beat in about 4 ozs. butter and 2 ozs. melted
chocolate.

For the caramel : 3 ozs. loaf sugar, 2 tablespoonfuls of
water. Boil until it becomes a rich brown caramel.

The rounds should be done in a medium oven and take
about 10 minutes to cook, but be careful not to overcook
them or they will break easily. The chocolate cream is
spread over each round and these are placed on top of each
other to form the cake. The caramel is poured over the
top round, only the sides are covered with the grated
chocolate.

A very pretty cake.

Gingerbread

HALF POUND flour, ½ lb. black treacle, ½ dessertspoonful ground ginger, ½ dessertspoonful mixed spice, ¼ lb. brown sugar, ¼ lb. fresh butter, ¼ teaspoonful bicarbonate of soda, ¼ pint milk, ½ oz. finely minced citron peel, 2 eggs.

Mix all the dry ingredients together. Warm the milk and let the butter slowly dissolve in it. Beat up the eggs and add with the treacle to the milk and butter, and stir in the dry ingredients. The mixture should be of a "runny" consistency (a thick butter). Add a little milk if necessary. Pour into a square cake tin not very deep and bake for ¾ hour. It should be a dark moist cake without crust.

N.B.—The gingerbread should be made 2 or 3 days before wanted and then cut into squares.

From Mrs. Engleheart

Lunch Cake

SIX OUNCES flour, 3 ozs. butter, 1 oz. Demerara sugar, 1 teaspoonful of ground ginger, 4 tablespoonfuls of black treacle, 2 eggs, chopped candied peel and some glacé cherries.

Rub the butter well into the flour, adding sugar, ginger and fruit. Then beat up the eggs and add. Melt the treacle until slightly warm, and add, and mix well.

Bake in a moderate oven for 1 to 1½ hours.

The Demerara sugar can be left out if thought too sweet.

Madeleines

TWO OUNCES BUTTER, 2 ozs. sugar, 1 egg, 2½ ozs. self-raising flour. Grate rind of lemon on to sugar, and then beat to a cream the sugar and butter, add egg and beat well into cream, and slowly add flour, beating well. Put into small buttered madeleine tins (which are made specially for the little cakes) and bake in a moderate oven. These cakes should be soft, not crisp, and it is done by not having the oven too hot.

Muffins

TAKE 1 LB. OF FLOUR. Mix 1 tablespoonful of baking powder, 1 saltspoonful of salt, ½ pint of sour milk.

Mix all together into a light dough, and stand it in a warm place to rise for ½ hour.

Then roll out in small rounds, place on a griddle for 10 minutes and brown both sides. Butter them well and serve very hot.

Rich Plum Cake

SIX OUNCES RAISINS, 6 ozs. peel, 8 ozs. currants, 4 ozs. sultanas or cherries, 4 ozs. powdered almonds, 8 ozs. bitter almonds.

Melt 7 ozs. butter, beat with 8 ozs. sugar till white, add 4 yolks of eggs, beating all the time. Have 8 ozs. flour warmed and sifted and mix with it 1 teaspoonful of ginger, quarter teaspoonful mixed spice and 1 teaspoonful of baking powder. Add this and 4 stiffly beaten whites of eggs. Mix flour and whites of eggs almost at same time, and lastly the fruit, over which a little of above flour has been thrown to prevent sticking together. Tie buttered paper high—moderate oven; takes from 2-4 hours.

Scotch Scones baked in Oven

HALF A POUND self-raising flour, 2 ozs. butter, pinch of salt. Put salt into flour, add the butter and mix well. Then add enough milk to make dough slack, not stiff. Cut into rounds and put on hot tin and bake in moderate oven.

Shortbread Biscuits

HALF A POUND flour, 6 ozs. butter, 1 oz. castor sugar. Rub all ingredients together till they form stiff dough ;

then roll out and cut into small rounds and bake in a moderate oven. When finished they should be quite light—not at all brown. Roll in castor sugar.

From Lady Brock

Very good and light Sponge Cake

FOUR EGGS, ¼ lb. of icing sugar, ¼ lb. flour, a good teaspoon of essence of lemon. Well beat the yolks of eggs, and the whites separately to a stiff froth, add whites to yolks and beat well together. Add the sugar by degrees, beating all the time, add lemon essence and the flour last and stir in lightly.

Bake in a *moderate* oven for ¾ hour.

The above makes a large cake that never gets dry.

From Lady Brock

South African Bun

For Afternoon Tea—Hot

TWO TEACUPFULS brown flour, 2 eggs, 1 teaspoonful of baking powder, ½ teaspoonful salt, 3 ozs. butter, ¼ cupful of milk, 2 tablespoonfuls sugar.

Mix flour, baking powder, sugar, salt and butter *dry* together. Add eggs and butter last. Put into cake tin and bake 1 hour.

Half this quantity for 1 bun (which serves 5 people).

Good Sultana Cake

LINE A CAKE TIN with 3 layers of greased paper. Cream together ¼ lb. butter and 6 ozs. castor sugar. Beat in 4 whole eggs : beat well between each one, adding by degrees ½ lb. flour to which 2 teaspoonfuls of baking powder have been added. Add the rind of 1 lemon and 4 ozs. of chopped mixed peel, and ¼ lb. sultanas. Bake in a moderate oven for about 1 hour.

Notes

Notes

Notes

SAVOURIES AND SALADS
For a Cocktail or After-dinner Savoury

BEAT UP A cream cheese with 2 tablespoonfuls of thick cream until very smooth. Add salt and pepper. Stone a dozen olives, mince very fine, mix up with the cheese and add a teaspoonful of minced green peppers. Either serve on rounds of brown bread buttered, or heap up on rounds of toast fried very crisp in butter.

Canapés

HAVE READY some fried or toasted bread cut into fingers.

Rub up sufficient butter with cayenne pepper, a few drops of lemon juice, and a drop or two of Tabasco, to spread on these fingers, and with the same mixture brush the same number of boned and filleted anchovies, and broil them for a minute or two until crisp. Dust with coralline pepper, place one on each finger, and serve as *hot as possible.*

Anchovy Fritters

POUND THE yolks of 2 hard-boiled eggs with half a dozen bottled anchovies, 1 teaspoonful of capers, 2 ozs. of butter, 1 tablespoonful of parsley, and 1 oz. of grated Parmesan cheese.

Rub all through a rather fine sieve, and add the yolk of a raw egg and 1 tablespoonful of fine breadcrumbs. Season with pepper, red pepper.

Form the paste into small rounds, roll first in breadcrumbs and then in egg, and again in crumbs, and drop into smoking hot fat. Fry a golden colour.

Serve on a napkin with grated Parmesan cheese.

Green Pea Sandwiches

(alternative to asparagus)

ABOUT ½ LB. OF pea purée to 6 ozs. thick cream. Boil peas in usual way, put through a sieve, season well; when cold stir thoroughly into the stiffly whipped cream. Roll small portions of this in thin brown or white bread and butter.

Herring Roes on Toast

MELT IN A saucepan a little butter. Put in the roes required. Cook well, mashing them up with a wooden spoon and whilst cooking add salt and pepper and a little drop of milk, but on no account let the roes get too liquid. After about 5 minutes they should be cooked. Then beat in a little thick cream. Pile the roes on pieces of hot buttered toast and serve very hot.

Iced Camembert Cheese

For 12 people

TAKE 2 FAIRLY RIPE Camemberts. Beat them up in a basin with some Tabasco sauce and a little salt. Add enough cream to make the mixture liquid—about 1 pint cream.

Put into a small flat tin—I have found the best that just holds this quantity is a tin that has had ice wafers in it. Put tin to freeze.

When quite frozen, cut into fingers and roll in grated Parmesan cheese, and coral of lobster, or coralline pepper will do.

Serve with mustard and cress in the middle of the dish, and send up plain hot crackers.

Old-fashioned Sardine Savoury

TAKE A SMALL or large tin of sardines according to

quantity required. Put through a coarse wire sieve and then make hot in a saucepan, adding a drop or two of anchovy essence and a drop of Tabasco. Have ready rounds of well buttered toast, pile your sardines on these, high in the centre, and pour over at the last minute the following melted butter sauce :

Take ½ pint of water, 1 oz. butter, ¾ oz. flour, salt and pepper. Having melted your butter in a saucepan stir in the flour and cook well for a few minutes, now add the water, which should be hot but not boiling; go on stirring continually until the sauce is absolutely smooth. Bring to the boil and then let simmer for a few minutes, *season* and pour over sardines. This savoury must be sent to table very hot, otherwise it will be a failure.

Savoury Biscuits

GRATE 2 OZS. Cheddar cheese, work into it 1 oz. butter, 1 teaspoonful each of anchovy and H.P. or similar sauce, a little made mustard, a sprinkle of cayenne pepper, very little salt. Make it quite a stiff paste. Put a small teaspoonful between 2 Carr's club cheese biscuits (about 2 of these for each person). Put in a moderate hot oven for 5 minutes. Serve at once.

Salads

I DO NOT PRETEND that these salad receipts are very original, but they are all ones that I constantly use myself.

Salad Dressing

ONE OF THE BEST salad dressings for a plain lettuce is the yolk of a hard-boiled egg mixed smooth with oil and

Tarragon vinegar, the usual salt and pepper and a little made mustard. When well mixed chop up the white of an egg and add to the dressing, or else shake it over the salad, and finish with some finely chopped taragon.

Salad I

A CRISP LETTUCE with $\frac{1}{4}$ pieces of hard-boiled egg laid on the leaves. The ordinary oil and vinegar dressing, or else a little whipped cream and lemon juice dressing, and a dust of coralline pepper on each piece of egg, makes a delicious and pretty salad for a cold meal.

Salad II

AN EXCELLENT salad is made with the very large dates that come into the market in the spring. Stone them and put a small piece of cream cheese inside each and serve on lettuce leaves with a well-mixed French dressing with paprika added to it.

French plums can be used in the same way, with or without the cheese filling.

Salad III

CELERIAC CUT THIN and long like matches, well soaked in water and drained, mixed with chopped apple (Newtowns are the best) to which you can add finely chopped walnuts. This makes a very good winter salad— mixed with cream and lemon juice dressing.

Salad IV

THE AVOCADO PEAR is quite one of the best salads when in season. Scoop out the fruit with a dessert spoon,

86

keeping the pieces whole. Lay in a salad bowl with lettuce leaves round, using a French dressing and paprika instead of ordinary pepper.

The avocado pear cut lengthways in half with the centre (whence the stone has been removed) filled with oil and vinegar dressing, and a half served to each guest, is really the best way to eat it. But as so many do not like the pear, it is better and not so wasteful to cut up the fruit as described.

Salad V

TAKE SOME skinned and stoned muscat grapes, sliced banana, and chopped nuts, all tossed in a French vinaigrette dressing, seasoned with pepper and salt.

Cauliflower Salad

ONE SO SELDOM sees a cold cauliflower salad in England, but in Italy they give you a young fresh cauliflower, boiled till tender (but not fallen to pieces). When drained and cold pour over it a good mayonnaise sauce, made with a little cream and lots of capers in it.

Chicory Salad

COLD CHICORY is excellent as a salad. Take large thick pieces and boil, keeping it very white (some milk added to the boiling water should do this). Let the chicory drain well for some hours and then pour a well-mixed oil and vinegar dressing (with a little paprika if liked) over it. French dressing cannot be made in a hurry. Ten minutes stirring is not in the least too long to make it really good.

Peach and Ginger Salad

TAKE A FEW bottled peaches cut in half, a little preserved

ginger, and some chopped-up walnuts. Make the dressing for this of whipped cream, a teaspoon of vinegar and a very little syrup of the ginger, and having put the fruit in centre of bowl, with a crisp white lettuce round, pour the dressing over and a little paprika dusted over. Leave out ginger syrup if considered too sweet.

Salad to serve with Fried Poussins

MAKE SOME gooseberry sauce by stewing as many as are required in as little water as possible, with the addition of a little sugar, and when soft pass through a sieve. Then stir over the fire with a small pat of butter, and flavour with just a pinch of ginger. Put this on ice, and when wanted have ready some large skinned tomatoes, cut in half, that have been well seasoned and soaked in oil and vinegar and put on ice. Pile up the iced gooseberry sauce on the halved tomatoes and put some nice lettuce leaves round. Serve with grilled poussins.

Notes

Notes

Index

93

Notes

Notes

Notes

For Product Safety Concerns and Information please contact our EU
representative GPSR@taylorandfrancis.com
Taylor & Francis Verlag GmbH, Kaufingerstraße 24, 80331 München, Germany

www.ingramcontent.com/pod-product-compliance
Lightning Source LLC
Chambersburg PA
CBHW050719280326
41926CB00088B/3312